Other Books by Don Lubov

Long Island Illustrated

Hyperspace

Long Island Zen – 1

Long Island Zen – 2

Who Am I and Why Am I Here?

Frosty The Soulman

Life's Purpose

The Six Step Path

Spirituality with a touch of Zen

Awaken Celebrate SIX-STEP PATH Observe Forgive Accept TO ENLIGHTENMENT Love

Zen

By

Don Lubov

The Six-Step Path

Spirituality with a touch of Zen

Copyright – 2013
by
Don Lubov

All Rights Reserved

Blog: Spiritshare.net

ISBN: 13: 978-1490398426

ISBN: 10: 1490398422

Printed in the U.S.A.

Dedication

To all those ready for the journey to
inner space. You won't be disappointed.
Here comes the real you. Prepare to witness
your own beautiful self.

You are part of something greater than yourself.

D.L.

Random Notes Explained

Content that I have labeled RANDOM NOTES are my comments on spirituality. Some are from a lecture given, some are a short comment to myself on spirituality. Some follow, directly, an article on a particular area of spirituality. Many are somewhat random. All are written to aid clarification.

Aphorisms

From the Fertile Crescent to Meso-America to Native-Americans to Asia and the West, aphorisms have been used to teach universal truths. They are concise, timeless and global.

*When you're through changing,
You're through.*
 Bruce Barton

Acknowledgements

Thanks to all prophets, sages and
bodhisattvas, past and present

Table of Contents

Aphorism 3	1
Introduction	2
Aphorism 4	3
Timeline	4
Aphorism 5	5
1971- My Enlightenment	6
Aphorism 6	9
Life's Purpose	10
Aphorism 7	11
Preface	12
Aphorism 8	14
Spirituality Manifesto	15
Aphorism 9	19
New Spirituality Introduction	20
Aphorism 10	23
Six-Step Path	24
Aphorism 11	26
School of Hard Knocks	27
Aphorism 12	31
Random Notes I	32
Aphorism 13	34
A Lifelong Craving	35
Aphorism 14	36
Summary & Liberation	37
Aphorism 15	40
Backdoor Fulfillment	41
Aphorism 16	43
Two Wolves	44
Aphorism 17	45
Spirituality & Zen	46
Aphorism 18	48
Random Notes II	49
Aphorism 19	51
Random Notes III	52
Aphorism 20	54
Surrender	55

Aphorism 21	56
12 Symptoms of a Spiritual Awakening	57
Aphorism 22	58
Random Notes IV	59
Aphorism 23	62
Random Notes V	63
Aphorism 24	65
Random Notes VI	66
Aphorism 25	67
Apples & Oranges	68
Aphorism 26	70
Gnostic Notes	71
Aphorism 27	72
Gnostic Timeline	73
Aphorism 28	74
Religion	75
Differences	76
Aphorism 29	78
Choice Number Three	79
Aphorism 30	82
Two Monks	83
Aphorism 31	84
Random Notes VII	85
Aphorism 32	87
Random Notes VIII	88
Aphorism 33	90
Random Notes IX	91
Aphorism 34	93
Random Notes X	94
Aphorism 35	96
Random Notes XI	97
Aphorism 36	98
Random Notes XII	99
Aphorism 37	102
Reminder	103
Aphorism 38	104
Happiness	105
Aphorism 39	107
Creativity	108
Aphorism 40	111

Inspirational Writing	112
Aphorism 41	114
Relationships – Do's & Don'ts	115
Aphorism 42	117
We are what we observe…	118
Aphorism 43	120
Meditation	121
Aphorism 44	122

Enlightenment is everybody's birthright.

                                                    D.L.

Introduction

In the beginning I was all there was. I was everything, including time itself. I was One. I wished to know myself. So, I pretended to separate into many I's. Through forgetfulness I made me (you) see you as a separate self. This false, temporary, separation, plus ego, helped you become lost in my physical, self-created, 3-D world of duality.

However, once lost, you could be found. When found, you again become conscious of your true identity of being the ALL; the One. But, having once been lost, you now have a greater understanding of what it means to be you. You now are grateful for and appreciate who you really are.

You were, are and always will be only One. There never will be a separate you. In fact, all the seemingly separate yous encountered along the way are also you. You are all there is, was and ever will be. You are formless and nameless and, you are love. Nothing else is real.

You asked yourself, before time, "Who am I?" You are the question and you are the answer. You are omnipotent, omnipresent and creative. You are All. You are not religion; which is exclusive. You are spirituality; which is inclusive. You are not belief; You are irrespective of belief. You are the greatest force in the universe – You are a force called LOVE...unconditional love.

You are a self in an eternal search of itself. You are your true self in disguise. You are the light you go towards. You are asleep but soon you will wake up...Wake up to the divinity in you. All journeys lead back home. Welcome to your reunion with you.

Spirituality is nonsectarian.
— D.L.

Timeline

13.7 billion BCE – universe begins (Big bang)
4.6 billion BCE – planet earth formed
1 million BCE – hominids appear
200,000 BCE – language begins – pre-Homo Sapiens
100,000 BCE – Homo Sapiens, language advances & fire mastered
20,000 BCE – global migration
10,000 BCE – settlements, agriculture (less land needed to feed each person)
5.000 BCE – Mesopotamia, Egypt, China ,the wheel
4,500 BCE – Jewish calendar begins
4,000 BCE - Uruk-(Iraq) – 50,000 people, Sumer (Mesopotamia) – first cities & government, writing, trade, politics, large-scale war
2,500 BCE – pyramids, Stonehenge, zigurats, Greece
1,400 BCE - Moses in Israel and Judaism
1,200 BCE – Iron Age, chariots
600 BCE – Zoroaster – monotheism, empires, Siddartha in India (Buddhism), Lao Tzu in China (Taoism), Confucius in China (Confucianism)
400 BCE – Old Testament
100 BCE - Mayan civilization
30 AD - Jesus (Joshua), Israel (Christianity)
67 AD - Bodhidarma brings dhyan to China (Ch'an)
200 AD - Aztec civilization
300 AD - Maitreya (first Bodhisattva)
325 AD - Constantine & Roman Catholicism, orthodox Christianity
600 AD - Mohammed, Arabia (Islam)
800 AD - Gunpowder
1200 AD - Inca civilization
1,227 AD - Dogen brings Cha'an to Japan (Zen)
1,600 AD - International trade, sugar/slavery in South America
1,700 AD - iron, coal, steam power, Industrial Revolution
1,800 AD - Europe rules
1,900 AD - oil, WWI, 1.6 billion people, D.T. Suzuki brings Zen to U.S. & West
2,000 AD - 7 billion people, energy-driven, Religious wars continue

Who forgives first, wins.
D.L.

1971-The Year of My Enlightenment

One day, while my friends were out food shopping, I stayed behind and relaxed in a big easy chair in the living room. I was wide awake and happy to be off the road. Except for me, the house was empty. It was quiet. In fact, it was more than just quiet. It was a surreal quiet. No usual sounds were to be heard. No birds chirping. No traffic noises. No talking or footsteps from people walking by. The quiet was so intense it made me wonder if it was possible to hear quiet. It was peaceful, too.

The clock on the mantle read twelve, noon. My concentration went from the all pervasive quiet to something rather startling. One by one, all the objects in the room were disappearing. They were replaced by a white nothingness, a comforting light.

The first to go was the clock on the mantle. Next was a picture on the wall. Then the nothingness swallowed up the entire mantle and fireplace. A wooden chair vanished in a split second. In a few more seconds, my world of three dimensions was completely gone. Nothingness even gobbled up the walls, the ceiling and the floor.

As if all this wasn't amazing enough, I was stunned with the realization that my body had also disappeared. All that was left of the me I had known for thirty years was my consciousness; wondering just what was happening. Strangely enough, there was no panic, just utter amazement at my situation.

All was calm. My consciousness just seemed to be floating in a beautiful, white, nothingness. I was bathed in this warm, not harsh, white light. I had no depth perception. It was almost like being in a cloud. There was nothing to focus on. Then I heard the voice. It was mezmerizing. I heard it even though I had no ears. I had to remind myself that I had no body, no head and, most assuredly, no ears. Yet, I had heard a voice.

It was a deep, soothing voice. It repeated, many times, "God is love" and "Love is God." I thought - *Does this mean that God loves me? and that I love God?* I'd never had a personal relationship with God. That is why I never had much to do with organized religion. For me, religion without spirituality was just so much ceremony. This was definitely not ceremony.

I'd always envied those who professed a personal connection to God. I knew it wasn't the kind of thing one could fake; either you had it or you didn't. Until now, I didn't. It was a personal connection to spirit; something greater than one's self. Hard to believe. Yet, what was happening now was as real as anything that had ever happened in my life. If this wasn't real, then nothing was real.

In answer to my query about whether God loved me or I loved God, the voice was quite specific. The voice said that there was no separate me to love God and no separate
God to love me. God and love were, and are, the same thing. Further, separation from God or spirit was only an illusion. All life and all spirit are connected, forever. Life's purpose is to wake up to this fact…to finally know one's true self.
Even now, forty-one years after this life-altering event, I get goose-bumps just thinking about it. I've never felt alone since this episode; never doubted its authenticity. Things happen when and where they are supposed to happen. There are no coincidences.

After what seemed like a long time, my consciousness realized that my friends would be returning soon, and this experience was not to be shared at this time. With this knowledge all of my three-dimensional world began to rapidly re-appear. The voice and light/nothingness faded away as objects returned. Even my body returned. Within a matter of seconds my old, conventional world was back and my new, non-physical world was gone. The clock on the mantle read 12:30,p.m., which meant that the entire incident had taken thirty minutes of what I now understood to be linear time.

I heard my friends approaching the front door. They entered and just stared at me. I must have had one heck of an expression on my face because all three of them asked what had happened to me. They said I looked awestruck--as though I'd seen a ghost. I certainly felt awestruck but, as instructed, I wasn't about to discuss it right now. I assured them that I had not seen a ghost. I'd just had an amazing thought and that it was time for me to move on...I'd be leaving in the morning.

Trust in that which does not change…that which is undetectable by the five senses.

D.L.

There is only one fundamental question –

Does life have a purpose?

If the answer is yes, then how you live your life matters. Your life would have meaning. The lives of others would have meaning.

If life does not have a purpose; if it is random, then how you live your life and how others live their lives becomes relatively meaningless.

How did we get here? Why this question at this time? Has this question always been of prime importance? Since we all come with expiration dates, there's not time to waste finding out.

Your true nature, who you truly are, is waiting to be uncovered.

D.L.

Preface

Only human beings are made in God's image. We can think and we know right from
Wrong. We were created to be like God. Is there a God?...Yes we are! As we let God
Into our life we are transformed from within. Your life is shaped by your thoughts.
Your trial and tribulations build character. There is a purpose behind every hardship. There are no coincidences.

Once born again you start becoming like the One who made you and your life becomes more beautiful. Change means fear and loss and pain. But, it also means growth.

You're here on earth to make a contribution. You're part of a mighty plan. You were created to contribute to life on earth. When you do that, you serve others. When you serve others you serve (God) yourself. Service and awakening go hand in hand. Once awakened you want to serve.

You were given abilities, interests, talents, gifts to develop and use…in service to others. Not using what you've been given is cheating the world of your gifts. Your heart tells you what you really care about, what you are passionate about, what you are enthusiastic about. Be mindful of what you love to do. Follow your passion and you will excel. The more you excel the better to serve while loving what you are doing.

Serving by doing what you love you experience fulfillment and satisfaction. Focus on your natural abilities and loves…the things you do when you lose track of time. You lose track of time and you feel fully alive.

It's not what happens to you that's important. It's what you do with what happens to you that's important; how you deal with what life hands you.

God wants to speak to the world through you.

Practice and develop your gifts and talents. Get lost in your life serving others. Learn from your life's lessons. Fix your gaze on that which is unseen…the eternal.

The heaviest thing to carry is a grudge. Forgiveness lightens the load.
D.L.

Spirituality Manifesto

Traditional religion can be a support system and moral guidepost for living in the outer, physical world. Spirituality, is the path to your inner world.

Traditional religion is external, formal, ritualistic and, above all, exclusive. It creates and "us verses them" mentality. It can cause competition and friction between religions. Spirituality is a nonsectarian path to enlightenment. It is the most important part of religion and works independently of religion. It leads to a personal relationship with spirit, nature, source, energy, God, etc. Universal cooperation is built in to spirituality.

Spirituality is the mystical experience of an individual that all too often leads to the formation of a religion by others...others who have not had this mystical experience. Preaching (sharing) universal truths need not lead to forming a religion. While religion puts information in you, spirituality uncovers what is already in you from birth; intuitively felt but not yet discovered.

Traditional religion needs followers. Spirituality needs nothing more than for you to lead yourself. Religion can be a comfort or a cause of discomfort. Spirituality can only comfort and offers a way to transcend the suffering of this world. Religion is filled with ritual and ceremony. Spirituality is spontaneous. Religion makes you dependent on it to intervene between you and God; to be your intermediary. Spirituality offers independence through direct contact with God. Salvation is a cornerstone of traditional religion. Spirituality, reveals that there is no need for salvation and makes you independent of everything.

With religion, your divinity is external and difficult to reach. With spirituality your divinity is within and well within reach. The religious God can be judgmental, angry and disappointed in you.

This is a God that craves obedience and loyalty. With spirituality, God is nonjudgmental, and has no need of your obedience or loyalty. This, true, inner God, is unconditional love.

Traditional religion is taught. No one is born knowing religion. It has to be learned. Religions can be very different...so anything can be taught. Spirituality is known, intuitively. It cannot be taught. It must be felt. It leads you to your beautiful, inner being; your true self.

There is more to you than meets the eye. Life is not random. It has a purpose. Life's purpose is a spiritual one – To know inner peace, you must make conscious contact with the spirit within you; which is undetectable by the five senses. And, you need to do this while still in your physical body. We all come with expiration dates, so there's no time to waste. Once this inner contact is made, how "successful" you are in the external, physical world, is no longer of prime importance.

Once your spirit, which is perfect, takes physical form, which is imperfect, it takes on flaws and weaknesses. It also takes on gifts and talents. All are unique to you. You are one in the universe with this particular combination. My **"Six-Step Path"** is designed to help you overcome your flaws and weaknesses and to encourage and make blossom your gifts and talents. This path guides you to channeling this creative spirit within to satisfying actions in the physical world.

To have a spiritual awakening, an epiphany, an enlightenment is a direct, prompt way to discover the meaning and purpose of life. It is so powerful and personal, it needs no outside validation; no stamp of approval. It is to be accepted as authentic.

Following such an event, you awaken to your connection to all life; especially all human life. It's clear – to serve others is to serve yourself and, vice-versa. This can be done in many ways, on all levels.

Freed from suffering, you transcend what Buddhists call "The Three Poisons" – Ignorance, Greed and Anger. Open, now, to your true, inner self, you encourage your unique gifts and talents (that we all have) to emerge and to blossom. This satisfies your very human need to express yourself in your particular way. It allows you to serve in a creative way.

Service to others brings peace of mind and a natural, effortless personal growth of talent or gift. Your satisfaction level soars. You know you're doing the right thing. Living through your special gifts, you become the best you you can be. All growth takes effort; work. But this "right" activity is so true and so honest that progress is assured and quick.

You are no longer part of the (human) problem. You glow with the knowledge that you are now part of the solution (to the human condition). You not only know what to do to express yourself and serve others but you are making wiser decisions on when and how to do it. It becomes effortless effort.

Your learned urge to compete morphs into an urge to cooperate. You see life through compassionate eyes...People first, all else second. Your self-reformation has united you with all life. Work is now joy and joy is your unique work.

In case you are one of many who have not had an epiphany; a spiritual awakening, not to worry. That is the "front-door" approach to finding meaning and purpose. There is an equally satisfying "back-door" approach to self-fulfillment.

Be still and non-judgmental and look within to see what it is that makes you truly happy. This is not necessarily only one thing, one activity. You may have multiple activities that please you. Explore with kindness, the inner you, the true you. Not what you've been taught to like or do, but what you honestly enjoy doing.

If it's your passion to sing, then "sing as though no one were listening. If it's your passion to dance, then dance as though no one were watching. And, as often as possible, love as though you've never been hurt." Discover what brings joy to you and begin to do it now. Do it, nurture it and share it. You will be sharing on a deep, spiritual level.

This focused, passionate living puts you in sync with the rest of the universe and creates a personal atmosphere conducive to enlightenment. When you live your true, inner self, your "divinity within" awakens and you begin living the life you are meant to live…your "enlightened" life.

This "back-door" approach is satisfying on all levels and builds on itself. As you get used to living your real self, your life gets better, your world gets better. You have fulfilled your destiny as a human being. You are in sync with the cosmos.

When you've got it all
and it's still not
enough, you're ready
for spirituality.

D.L.

New Spirituality Introduction

For most of the past 100,000 years, the purpose of life for homo sapiens has been to survive, physically, in a hostile environment. Shamefully, that singular purpose is still the same for most people alive today. Full-time hunting and gathering continues to be the main means of survival for most of the world. This is usually a group effort. The tribe's survival depends on the involvement of the entire community.

There was an important change about 9,000 years ago, when agriculture (farming) was begun. This change in life style allowed people all over the world to stop wandering. Transient campsites evolved into settlements, towns and cities. With excess crops came commerce (selling excess produce) and craft trades. This was not a group effort. This meant wealth for a few at the expense of many and was the start of capitalism. The privileged few could now entertain leisure and non-physical ventures.

Until approximately 6,000 years ago, religion was polytheistic. Zoroaster, in Persia (present day Iran), was the first to introduce monotheism. Sages and prophets have been passing on these teachings, orally, ever since. From 3,500B.C.E. on, these universal truths have been shared by written texts as well.

Regardless of time or place, teachings that have to do with life, death and the impermanence and suffering of existence have been universally accepted. The goal of freedom from all kinds of suffering is paramount. The transformation from a fear-based existence to one of love is imperative. Enlightenment, epiphany and spiritual awakening – these are the ultimate achievements. This transformation from a life of pain to one of peace, love and joy is the seekers reward.

The spiritual awakening is here and now...not at some future time or place. It is proof that life does have a purpose and that purpose is a spiritual one. Although religions may differ in their ritual and ceremony, spirituality consistently offers the same wise advice – basically The Golden Rule, in one form or another. Through various types of formal meditation, the seeker arrives at an intuitive understanding of life and its purpose.

The awakened understanding is beyond thought. It is non-intellectual and not detectable by the five senses. It is, however, detectable by the sixth sense; the intuition. This is understanding through feeling. It is a direct, personal experience that lasts a lifetime.

You study yourself to find your inner self; your true self. The only thing given up in this spiritual quest for identity is your ego. It, like all else on this physical, three-dimensional plane, is temporary. All here is ruled by the law of change. This world of duality – hot-cold, up-down, rough-smooth, beginnings and ends, birth and death, is transient and illusion. Once you connect, consciously, with the only permanency in an impermanent world, you know, down to your bones, that you have found something truly real. It is not only real, it is the eternal singularity…not like anything experienced before.

Formal meditation involves ritual and ceremony. It has to be taught. It has to be learned. This takes time and effort. There is only here and only now. All else is illusion. The choice of whether or when to awaken to this is yours and yours alone. Free will prevails. A new you, a new understanding, a new life awaits you. All you have to do is be still and do nothing.

There is, however, an alternative to formal meditation. It has no ritual, no ceremony and is informal, relatively quick and user-friendly. You become "mindful" (aware) of your life as it is happening. Your life becomes your meditation with my "Six-Step Path". Almost effortlessly, you learn to *Observe, Forgive, Accept, Love, Awaken and Celebrate.*

All spiritual paths lead to the same place. All of history's sages offer the same, wise advice. Try a variety of paths. Find one that's right for you. You're entitled to two births. The first is physical. The second is spiritual. If you try, you'll succeed. You are programmed for success.

> "The world isn't so much as we find it but as we make it."
>
> Anonymous

The Six-Step Path

Step 1. **Observe** yourself without judgment
Step 2. **Forgive** yourself and others.
Step 3. **Accept** what you observ
Step 4. **Love** yourself unconditionally.
Step 5. **Awaken** from your dream.
Step 6. **Celebrate** life forever.

As Siddartha and many others and others have made clear for the past 2,500 years—"All life is suffering". Fortunately, he and others offer ways to transcend this suffering. The way is meditation...not necessarily formal meditation. The form of meditation I endorse is informal...It is your daily life..."as it is".

At first, the Six-Step Path may seem simplistic. Actually, it is—we are complex. Socrates was so right when he said—"The unexamined life is not worth living".

My Six-Step Path begins with **Observation**...not just any observation. This most difficult of all six steps is non-judgmental observation. With non-judgmental observation you witness your own behavior with all its flaws and weaknesses that all humans possess.

For example, when you get angry, observe that anger. Focus your attention on it. Don't judge it as either justified or wrong or any other qualifier. Simply see it as a behavior of you, a human being. The more intense and often you focus your attention on your behavior...all your behaviors, without judgment, the more you will see these behaviors begin to wane. The more you see the less they will be. As you get more familiar with your true, imperfect self, you will become, little-by-little, more forgiving of your real self.

This brings us to the second step in the Six-Step Path...That of **Forgiveness.** The degree to which you judge yourself is the degree to which you judge others. As you begin to lighten up and be more forgiving of yourself...your own flaws and weaknesses, your judgment of others will also become less frequent and less harsh. In time, this forgiveness of your self and others leads to step three of the Six-Step Path—**Acceptance.**

Once you can observe without judgment and forgive imperfections you naturally adopt an attitude of acceptance. To forgive and accept what you observe, in yourself and others, is the beginning of true spirituality...and, ultimately, enlightenment.

Living a non-judgmental life of observation, forgiveness and acceptance brings you to the fourth step in the Six-Step Path—**Love**. Unconditional love; love without conditions; for your self and others. This is the true, and only, love that comes from our source, through us, to all life. This love IS our source (and us). At this point you are in sync with your source...no longer trying to control the world, just letting it be. In Zen this is "life as it is".

Living in this manner you will surely **Awaken** from your dream—your dream of separation from your source into a separate, ego-centered identity. Your awakening; also called: satori, enlightenment, epiphany, etc. is two-fold—First you know, down to your bones, that you are part of something greater than yourself. Next, you realize that you ARE that thing greater than yourself.

When this happens, you can't help but want to **Celebrate** every moment of life for the miracle it is. The way to express this understanding is to serve others; for they are you...All life is one. Celebrate life forever.

As you progress (imagined) from being a fear-based, ego-centric part of the universal problem, you become an accepting, loving, part of the solution. Your self in search of itself has found itself in six steps. You are now back where you started but with the understanding of what it means to be...who you are and where you are...in the now.

> *"Although the world is full of suffering, it is also full of overcoming it."*
> — Helen Keller

The School of Hard Knocks

It's been said, over and over, that we are physical beings who live in a world where a very few of us might get lucky and have a spiritual experience. In truth, we are spiritual beings who are temporarily having a physical experience.

As spirit, we are immortal, eternal and are aware of our connection to all life -- something greater than ourselves. We are also formless. However, to grow, spiritually, we must take physical form. When we do this, we temporarily give up our awareness of our connection to all life, our knowledge of our immortality and of the unconditional love of which we art part. We also forget that our non-physical being is perfect.

Why would we do this? Why pretend to give up a perfect life for one of imperfection? The reason is to grow spiritually – We can only become enlightened when in the physical form. Imperfect? Yes. But necessary and worth the effort. This is how we answer our eternal question to ourselves: "Who Are we?"... "Who am I?"

For the first six months of our lives we are more in touch with our spirit nature than our physical world. From this early age we begin to have an ego. Through the ego we begin to feel a separation from our spiritual life and begin to get attached to our physical world. We are becoming an "I", no longer a "we".

None of this would work without the element of forgetfulness. To get lost in our world of form we must forget our true, formless, world of spirit. And, we do. We do it so well that most of us believe, for the rest of our physical lives, that the physical world, the world of form, is all there is.

When we experience something abnormal; like déjà vu or an out-of-body event, we either discount it as an aberration to be ignored or something to be frightened of. We are trained to be stressed if we ever hear inner voices that others do not hear. Either way, anything that threatens our "normal", physical existence, is to be denied.

This is not a bad state of affairs. This is necessary. As the song "Amazing Grace" says:
"I once was lost but now I'm found." – To be found one must first get lost. Our school of hard knocks is designed to help us get lost. We inhabit a world of duality – up/down, black/white, yin/yang, male/female. Everything in this world is dual and subject to the law of change.

So, here we are; a perfect being in an imperfect form, in a world of duality subject to the law of change. We have forgotten our true, eternal, origin of unconditional love and are becoming more and more attached to this three-dimensional, mortal, physical world of form. All is working as it should.

To know yourself you must know others. To know what it means to have more you must know what it means to have less. To know ease you must learn to struggle and so on with peace/war, pleasure/pain, success/failure and so on. No coin has only one side. To know life you must have an understanding of both sides.

If there were no up, where would down begin? No hot, where would cold begin? These are not opposites, they are complements. They are each part of the other. It's a package deal. To have one you must have the other.

Hear the funniest joke ever and you can laugh just so long...change rules. Experience a sadness beyond belief and you must eventually stop crying...change rules. Just like the weather and the seasons, whatever is happening now will change...change rules. You are changing whether you want to or not...change rules. You are immersed in a world of change searching for that which does not change...for that which has no beginning and therefore, no end...that which, being eternal, has no birth and so has no death.

In a relatively short time we become attached to this world of duality. It may be frightening, tough and painful at times but, due to the law of change, these lead us to happy and joyful times, too. All is temporary. Once we realize that change rules we can weather all storms of dismay as they happen. When we decide that this game of pretend has gone on for long enough we begin to wonder – *"Is this all there is?"* At this point the conscious, earnest search for our true self begins.

Our imagined journey is not from point A to point B. It is from point A to point A only, with learning, we get back to point A and know it for the first time. We never really go anywhere but we do get to learn. This is the school of hard knocks. We learn and, due to "free will", we learn in our own time.

We go from being (unknowingly) part of the problem; operating from a position of fear, to being part of the solution; operating from a position of love. Just as darkness is the absence of light, fear is the absence of love...Not real absence, only perceived absence. We can never really be separate from our Source of unconditional love...but we can think we are. We can perceive ourselves as being separate blades of grass but we are all part of the lawn.

Now, part of the solution, we work to help others to learn what we have learned. Why? Because we now know that they are us. We are all connected and part of the same thing greater than ourselves. We know that we are the light we go towards. With this remembering that our true self is eternal, we lose our fear of death...What has a beginning must have an end...That which has a birth must have a death. We are eternal.

Having come full circle, from point A to point A, we have fulfilled our destiny as a human being; of going from being everything to thinking we were less than everything, to knowing, down to our bones, that we are everything. Our forgetfulness gone, although still in human form, we are awareness of spirit in a physical body. We have made conscious contact with the divinity within. This is what we call enlightenment, epiphany, satori, spiritual awakening.

We are now free from suffering, off the wheel of karmic debt, able to live a spontaneous life, in the moment...awake, alert and without thought. When awake, alert and without thought...not thinking, we are in meditation. When in meditation we are no longer self-directed. When not self-directed, we are Source-directed...what we call God takes over. We are one with the universe. We do what we love and we love what we do. Life becomes effortless.

Sad things still happen, but suffering ends. We embrace all life, as it happens, now. We are ready, willing and eager to serve others.

Being awake, alert and without thought ...and without judgment, ends stress and leads to enlightenment.

D.L.

Random Notes I

Your physical, 3-D world of duality and all its events are your path to spiritual awakening. Everything that has happened in your life was necessary for you to be where you are now…curious about God and the purpose of life…,to awaken to the divinity within and to express that divinity; in your own, unique way.

You soul wishes to remember what it knows; its divine nature. Once remembered, it wishes to experience what it knows. It does this by expressing, on the physical plane, this knowledge. We are all born with unique gifts and talents. As we develop them and become skilled with them, we are prepared to use them in the name of true inspiration.

In all these things, happenings, etc., trust your heart and intuition…your feelings. They will not lead you astray. Feelings lead to thoughts which lead to words which lead to action. The soul feels. The mind thinks. The body acts. As you feel and think, so things shall be; on the physical plane.

Discovering your oneness with all life is what life is all about. Part One of your awakening, epiphany, enlightenment, etc. is realizing that you are part of something greater than yourself. Part Two is realizing that you ARE that thing greater than yourself.

"to miss the mark"; not s"original sin" - new testament, an old archery term. "he who has achieved his aim" – Siddartha

"to learn to live with things "as they are".

By claiming to be a victim one gets out of taking responsibility for one's actions. Your only power is over yourself. Sheldon Kopp

"…to deny love is to deny God."

…we all want to belong to something greater than ourselves.

"…he becomes a lonely, wayfarer, a back-packing, foot-sore, simple, honest man – a man on a journey – a Holy Warrior. " Sheldon Kopp

"enlightenment does not provide perfection. Instead it simply offers the possibility of living with the acceptance of imperfection. One must learn to find the joy in the world "as it is."…in every hour of every day…the joy of everyday life.." Kopp

Purpose make suffering bearable.

"The secret is that there's no secret." Stop questioning and surrender to your everyday existence – When hungry, eat; and when you are tired, sleep.

You are already (and always have been) a Buddha. Just recognize (to identify as previously known) this, accept it and be content. There's nowhere to go and no one to be.

Don't try to change the "nature of things" or to control others. All answers lie within. Our freedom lies within. Our meaning lies within. Our divinity lies within.

Don't ask permission to be you, but do take responsibility for your actions. And, do your best.

The less you want,
the more you have.
D.L.

A Lifelong Craving

Have you noticed that no matter how much external success people have, they may still not be happy. They can have everything going for them – youth, looks, good physical health, connections, power, talent, money and fame. Still, they squander all this on booze, drugs and suicide.

We're perplexed. We wonder how they can do this? Why throw all these gifts and good fortunes away? Will they ever be content? Will they ever be happy and at peace? What do they really want? What do they need?

It must be something that can't be satisfied by more...more money, more fame, more career success. They are on an opulent merry-go-round of more. More of the same just will not do. They are living proof that no amount of material success will bring inner peace. No matter how much external success possessed, it cannot be a substitute for inner peace. When you're thirsty, food will not do...You need water. When you're tired, a new car will not do. You need rest.

So, what they're craving must be something different from these obvious attainments...When hungry for love, a new house or big business deal will not do. Unconditional love is what we crave from birth and, when recognized as eternally present within us, we can relax and enjoy whatever level of external success we have.

And, the good news is that unconditional love is not something you attain. It is not something you work for. It is a given...from birth. It is already within. It is something you uncover/discover. It is already there.

*I and want, what a pair.
I and not want, no stress there.*

D.L.

Summary and Liberation

Separation from the divine (within) leads to suffering from no sense of value, no meaning and no purpose to life.

In this state, people know intuitively that there is more to life than they are currently experiencing. Consequently, in their search for this (ineffable) something more, they turn to religion, philosophy and spirituality.

In a world of fear, doubt and impermanence, people want love, security and permanence. You either attempt to escape from this (temporary), egotistical world through drugs, sex, alcohol, extreme behaviors, etc. or you begin a conscious search for your (spiritual) roots.

For any of the following reasons, the search for peace and understanding begins –
Curiosity, Worry, Injustice, Violence, Anger, Fear Guilt, Grief, Doubt, Death and suffering of all kinds. The search is for a world of Love, Kindness, Compassion, Peace, Safety and Happiness and Fulfillment.

Such a world is achievable, by all, in the here and now...a world of value, meaning and purpose. It is not only achievable, it is your destiny.

Sages throughout history have offered transformational solutions to this sad state of affairs. People such as: Jesus, Hillel, Confucius, Socrates, Lao Tzu, Plato, Aristotle, Moses, Zoroaster and Siddartha. From 3,000B.C. on, these prophets have offered paths to open consciousness and to awaken people to their full potential. Their teachings come from personal experience and are offered for consideration and testing.

Basically, they all come down to practicing the Golden Rule. Just this one universal truth could change our world for the better. We just need to treat others as we wish to be treated. To transcend suffering and go on to enlightenment we only need to accept the physical world as it is – impermanent and full of all kinds of suffering.

Just as Adam and Eve had to leave (paradise) the Garden of Eden to experience the pain and death of the physical world, we must do the same...not avoidance but acceptance.

By experiencing this acceptance of things as they are, we earn the right to transcend them. You are not static. You are in flux and can, and must, change. In fact, you live in a world ruled by the law of change – the time of day, the seasons, your body, your health, your relationships, your age, etc. are all subject to change.

Buddha, Jesus, Confucius and others delivered a message of liberation and transcendence. They were all messengers of good news and were to be listened to, but not worshiped..."Follow the message, not the messenger." These prophets were all living proof that transformation is possible for all. Not only possible, but mandatory. This is our destiny and our purpose.

Heaven, nirvana, paradise, etc. is to be found here and now, by all. You only need to know where and how to look. There is (internal) perfection in this (external)imperfect, physical world. There is a larger, greater, deeper, permanent you waiting to be uncovered. It is within your grasp. This hidden, but attainable you, is undetectable by your five senses. However, It can be felt by your sixth sense; your intuition.

It is our natural, healthy state. It is nameless, but has been called: God, Allah, Energy, Source, Universal Force, Cosmic Consciousness, It, The Absolute and more. It is inside all of us waiting for our conscious contact. With this contact, you become the best you you can be. You begin to live the life you are meant to live...a life of peace, love and joy. You learn to serve others as you serve yourself.

You do what you love and love what you do. Your life will have meaning and purpose.

Familiarize yourself with the sages and prophets mentioned here. Try out their teachings and see if they work in your life. As a user-friendly, easy guide from stress to enlightenment I offer my own "Six-Step Path" – 1. Observe yourself without judgment. 2. Forgive yourself and others. 3. Accept what you observe. 4. Love yourself unconditionally. 5. Awaken from your dream. 6. Celebrate life forever. For more information, please see my blogsite: Spiritshare.net.

My "Six-Step Path" shows you how to transform your life into your own (informal) meditation. It is a relatively quick, effortless path to liberation and transformation. It has worked for thousands and can work for you.

All behaviors come from either love or fear.
D.L.

Backdoor Fulfillment

To have a spiritual awakening, an epiphany, an enlightenment is a direct, prompt way to discover the meaning and purpose of life. It is so powerful and personal it needs no outside validation; no stamp of approval. It is to be accepted as authentic and real.

Following such an event, you awaken to your connection to all life; especially all human life. It's clear – to serve others is to serve yourself and, vice-versa. This can be done in many ways, on all levels.

Freed from suffering, you transcend what the Buddhists call "The Three Poisons" – Ignorance, Greed and Anger. Open, now, to your true, inner self, you encourage your unique gifts and talents (that we all have) to emerge and to blossom. This satisfies your very human need to express yourself in your particular way. It allows you to serve in a creative way.

Service to others brings peace of mind and a natural, effortless personal growth of talent or gift. Your satisfaction level soars. You know you're doing the right thing. Living through your special gifts, you become the best you you can be. All growth takes effort; work. But this "right" activity is so true and so honest that progress is assured and quick.

You are no longer part of the (human) problem. You glow with the knowledge that you are now part of the solution to the human condition. You not only know what to do to express yourself and serve others but you are making wiser decisions on when and how to do it.

Your learned urge to compete is morphing into an urge to cooperate. You see life through compassionate eyes...People first, all else second. Your self-reformation has united you with all life. Work is now joy and joy is your unique work.

In case you are one of many who have not had an epiphany; a spiritual awakening, not to worry. That is the "front-door" approach to finding meaning and purpose. There is an equally satisfying "back-door" approach to self-fulfillment.

Be still and non-judgmental and look within to see what it is that makes you truly happy. This is not necessarily only one thing, one activity. You may have multiple activities that please you. Explore with kindness, the inner you, the true you. Not what you've been taught to like or do, but what you honestly enjoy doing.

If it's your passion to sing, then "sing as though no one were listening. If it's your passion to dance, then dance as though no one were watching. And, as often as possible, love as though you've never been hurt." Discover what brings joy to you and begin to do it now. Do it, nurture it and share it. You will be sharing on a deep, spiritual level.

This focused, passionate living puts you in sync with the rest of the universe and creates a personal atmosphere conducive to enlightenment. When you live your true, inner self, your "divinity within" awakens and you begin living the life you are meant to live...your "enlightened" life.

This "back-door" approach is satisfying on all levels and builds on itself. As you get used to living your real self, your life gets better, your world gets better. You are in sync with the cosmos.

Learning from one's mistakes is what makes them worthwhile.

D.L.

Two Wolves

One evening an old Cherokee told his grandson of a battle that goes on inside people. He said: "My son, the battle is between two wolves inside all of us. One is evil. It is anger, jealousy, regret, sorrow, self-pity, greed, arrogance, guilt, resentment, lies, inferiority, false pride, superiority and ego. The other is good. It is love, hope, peace, joy, serenity, kindness, humility, faith, empathy, benevolence, generosity and compassion." The grandson thought about this and then asked the grandfather: "Which wolf wins?" The old Cherokee replied: "The one you feed."

Anonymous

Except for now, all is change.
　　　　　　　　D.L.

Spirituality With a Touch of Zen

God, energy, cosmic consciousness, universal force, Allah, source, Yaweh, are some of the names given to a force undetectable by out five senses. Undetectable, but as real as anything else in our lives. However, it is detectable by our sixth sense; our intuition.

It is our number one job, as inquiring sentient beings, to make conscious contact with this force while still in our physical bodies. If we do not do this, we will never know complete inner peace. This applies to all of us; including our multi-successful celebrities. Fortunately for us, this is doable. Not only is it doable, but we are programmed for success in this endeavor. It is our destiny…our purpose.

Making contact with this source; our divinity within, in no way interferes with our other, more materialistic pursuits. "Before enlightenment, chop wood and carry water. After enlightenment, chop wood and carry water". This contact strengthens us in all directions and encourages our inner, true selves to emerge and to blossom. Making this inner connection is not as difficult as you might think. There is a guide for accomplishing this.

It can be done surprisingly quickly, with a high degree of success. The guide I am referring to is my "Six-Step Path". It has worked for thousands of people, just like you. It teaches you how to make your life, as it is happening, your meditation.

The goal of all meditation is to get us in a state where we are awake, alert and without thought. This is not that unusual. We do it all the time. We get lost in the moment; the now of our lives on a regular basis – We get lost in movies, books, hobbies, sports, socializing. We have many "right activities" uniquely tailored to our inner selves. They begin early and can change over time.

Siddartha, Jesus, Moses, LauTsu, Mohammed, et. al. Repeated the same phrase: "Life is suffering". You can transcend all suffering and begin the life you deserve: one of peace, love and joy. As Abe Lincoln said: "Most people are about as happy as they make up their minds to be".

Life is not so much as you find it but as you make it. Nasty people attract nasty people. Loving people attract loving people…cause and effect, karma. My "Six-Step Path" gives you the tools to enlightenment. It's up to you to use them. A new, fulfilling life awaits you. You can be the best you you can be, 24/7. You can be at peace. The choice, as always, is yours.

Attitude is everything.
    D.L.

Random Notes II

Religion, in its pure form, and spirituality are compatible, However, once religion focuses on power and politics, they become incompatible; no longer in sync with each other.

In an uncertain (physical) world, people feel an intellectual and emotional need for certainty. One can choose to satisfy this need by dogma or fundamentalism, but neither of these secures a comfortable, permanent reality.

Sometimes called God, nirvana, tao, Brahmin, there is a reality behind the one we can see with our eyes. It is not detectable by our five senses. It is, however, detectable by our sixth sense; our intuition. It is a dimension that one transcends to when thought reaches the end of its rope. It is beyond thought. It is the destiny of all human beings to reach this consciousness.

Silence is the path to it. Non-doing is the path to it. No-self is the path to it. Being mindful of the present moment is the path. This is not a place for human doings...It is the place for human beings. The same sages, prophets and gurus who claim that this is the only place to dwell, point the way to it. In a world of suffering, it is the only desirable place to be.

It is a place of unconditional love, peace and joy. It is home to the "Golden Rule" mentioned by Jesus, Confucius, Moses, Mohammed, Lao Tsu, Hillel and others. It is where God dwells and it is within (all of us). God and love are the same. Find one and you have found the other.

It is a graduation from the three poisons of Buddhism – "Ignorance, greed and anger." Compassion rules here and the rule of the law of change does not apply here. Once here, all good teachings pass through you into the physical world. Your daily life becomes your meditation (informal). You feel a connection to all life, especially other people.

When you allow your intuition, not your intellect, to lead you, you welcome this higher consciousness into your life. You are using that part of you that usually lies dormant. Trust your heart and your intuition. Follow your feelings.

The external, physical, 3-dimensional world (of duality), that we are most used to is not quite as reliable as you might think. It is subject to change on a regular basis and, as Heisenberg says in his "principle of indeterminancy" in quantum physics, physical reality is neither objective nor fixed. Faith, belief and subjectivity play a major role in choosing one's reality.

The world is how we make it, not how we find it. This gives us awesome power and, simultaneously, equally awesome responsibility. Believe it or not – We are the world.
With spirituality (spiritual awakening, epiphany, enlightenment, etc) it is possible to live in a world of suffering, pain, anger, injustice, violence and death lovingly, joyfully and peacefully. Through silence and surrender, to a world beyond words, we achieve everlasting peace.

This is not only doable, it is essential. We are programmed for success. Our birthright is two-fold; Our first birth is physical. Our second is spiritual. Embrace your whole humanity...the intellectual and the spiritual. Become part of the (human) solution and no longer part of the (human) problem. It is your destiny to live a life of peace, love and joy and to be the best you you can be.

In this 21st century, become a "homo-spiritualis".

Ignorance is not bliss.

Ignorance is pain…

Innocence is bliss.

D.L.

Random Notes III

Nothing exists outside of God, Source, spirit, etc. God is everything and so wants and needs nothing.

Man created God is his own image. Just look within and remember.

The link between man's spirit and God is faith; born of spirit, not flesh...not detectable by the five senses. Feelings are the language of the soul.

Thoughts lead to words which lead to reality (The Law of Creation). Create the desired event within to make it happen outside. Create a picture in your mind and see it as having happened...and feel it. Consciously create your own reality. Ideas lead to thoughts which lead to feelings which lead to reality. Trust your feelings...your intuition and your heart.

Law of Causality – What you do, how you behave comes back to you. (Life is an echo. What you send out comes back. Old Chinese proverb).

You are responsible for your own thoughts and actions. Now. Now is the only time there is. Life is now. Life is precious – all life. Life is One.

God, life, etc. is a creative power that exists within all of us.

Your new life begins now. You and God are not separate, nor have you ever been.

You are what you seek. You are the question and the answer. You are the light you go towards. The way to find your true, loving self is by serving others and loving others...for they are you. All is truly One. This is how Source learns to know itself and to express its true self...which is love.

Living your life as it is meant to be lived; which brings you joy, is a constant celebration of life with love. Whichever behavior or path makes it possible to experience your connection to the Divine and to express yourself creatively is the right one for you.

Life happens through you, not to you. First – belief. Second – behavior.

We think our soul yearns to be re-united with its Source, God, etc. In fact, it is always united with Source. By seeking something we already have, we deny having it.

God is both the creator and the created. One with all. Life itself.

Lose your ego and you lose yourself... only to gain the world.

D.L.

Surrender

Spiritual surrender is essential, whether on a religious or non-religious path. This kind of surrender is a joyous submission...to something greater than yourself. It comes with a conscious connection to your source...within. You trade external, intellectual, egoistic control for internal, loving, spiritual control.

Acknowledging your connection to your "greater" self is a willing servitude. Humility, gratitude and compassion replace money, status and material success as life's main goals.

This new mindset transcends all beliefs and faiths with a deep knowing down to your bones. Desire and attachment fall by the wayside. Life as it presents itself, in the moment, becomes the preferred lifestyle. Stress and suffering disappear. All is calm and as it should be.

As your life becomes your (ongoing) meditation, your awareness of yourself and your surroundings grows. The school of hard knocks is open 24/7. For those open to it; learning abounds. To study and become aware of yourself is to, eventually, forget yourself. To forget yourself is to become enlightened.

Energy, cosmic consciousness, universal force, It, God, source, the One, is all there is...to be seen everywhere.

Be one hundred percent involved and zero percent attached.

D.L.

12 Symptoms of Spiritual Awakening

1. An increased tendency to let things happen rather than make them happen.
2. Frequent attacks of smiling.
3. Feelings of being connected with others and nature.
4. Frequent overwhelming episodes of appreciation.
5. A tendency to think and act spontaneously rather than from fears based on past experience.
6. An unmistakable ability to enjoy each moment.
7. A loss of ability to worry.
8. A loss of interest in conflict.
9. A loss of interest in interpreting the actions of others.
10. A loss of interest in judging others.
11. A loss of interest in judging self.
12. Gaining the ability to love without expecting anything.

Anonymous

"Live in such a way that those who know you but don't know God will come to know God because they know you."

Anonymous

Random Notes IV

Spirituality was never the problem of the masses. But religion and politics can be.

Science rejects any hypothesis that is not based on the human experience in the physical world and therefore cannot be tested. Yet, spiritual truth is based on human experience...of the sixth sense. If something can neither be proven to be true nor false does not render it unworthy.

The more rigid a belief system or movement, the more it's based on fear.

From the 1870's to the present, science and religion have been at odds. In 1925, the Scopes trial was a contest between evolution and creation; between science and religion, not between science and spirituality. Spirituality and religion are NOT synonymous. Spirituality is neither religion nor science and can bridge the gap between these two warring parties.

Enlightenment comes from or leads to a constant, daily "mindfulness". It transcends both belief and faith. While many of us can do without religion, none of us can do without spirituality. If your only beliefs are with science and the five-sense areas, technology and money with no connection to spirit, you may never know complete, inner peace. You may never know what it means to be truly human.

The Holocaust came about from what Karen Armstrong calls: "soulless technocrats"...people with no sense of the sacred. A belief in or experience with something greater than one's self is necessary to give meaning to life. Almost any form of meditation can lead to this, even informal meditation.

Neither spirituality nor art is rational and should not be subject to rational scrutiny. One's ultimate being; one's inner self, is not to be understood by the mind, but must be felt, intuitively. God or spirit (not religion) is not something you grasp. It is something you feel, something you discover within. With this uncovering, the void or emptiness disappears and questions of your existence are resolved. You transcend the self and become connected to all life. The source within that is fundamental to our existence, is revealed. This is you without ego.

Life needs to have meaning and purpose. Otherwise, despair, depression and anger prevail. Practicing the behavior of a sage or guru daily can lead to a spiritual transformation. If you mimic your hero or heroine, you can become like them.

Different faiths, different rituals and different cultures can interpret reality differently and they can all be correct. To be open to that which is not rational; love, art, poetry, spirituality, we have to open up in a non-intellectual way. Transcendence is of the intuitive realm, the feeling realm; not the reasoning realm.

Human experience, in general, is of the mind and , therefore, open to interpretation and, to some degree, unreliable. Knowledge, with few exceptions, is subjective...See quantum mechanics. The world is not so much as we find it but as we make it. This results in equal portions of power and responsibility.

To paraphrase Karen Armstrong again:– "Originally, religion had the job of helping us live creatively, peacefully and joyously...as we do with art. It also can help us cope with mortality, pain, grief, despair, injustice and cruelty and, facing an uncertain future. Between rationality and the transcendent is unknowing. Unknowing alerts us to listen receptively and without judgment. God lies beyond words and concepts, yet can be felt. God is not a fact, a thing, but a presence, to be experienced. It is active, not static and, ultimately, ineffable."

"Existence is suffering" is the first noble truth of Buddhism. Spirituality is a way to transcend all suffering and go on to a life of peace, love and joy...as we are intended to live. We are all born with gifts and talents. These gifts and talents need room to breathe and to blossom. We can create a nonjudgmental, healthy, inviting atmosphere for them to emerge and thrive. Holiness is within, now. You can live intensely, passionately and richly, now, in your daily life. Enlightenment is your birthright and your destiny.

God is love and love is God.

D.L.

Random Notes V

Religion makes us aware of God. Spirituality allows us to transform our lives and give it purpose. It puts us in touch with God. Religion can be a guide. Spirituality makes you your own guide. Religion is a bridge to God. Spirituality is union with God.

"With spirituality you embrace the world, melt into god and become the love that is God." Spirituality takes us beyond religion to awareness of the sacredness in all; here and now, always. Religion is about God. Spirituality is a personal connection to God.

Our essence, our source, etc. is the subject of religion. This essence leads us to the sacredness of all life. The sacred, the secular, the material, the spiritual are all part of the One. Religion itself is not sacred…It is a path to the sacred. It is not the destination.

Spirituality is the Zen in Zen Buddhism. You are the creator and witness of all that is. You are the question and the answer. You are a self in search of itself. You are perfect, as is. You just need to wake up to it. Everything you need to know has been in you since birth.

Meditation of all kinds leads to transcending suffering and to a life of peace, love and joy. Informal meditation is easier and quicker.

God is love and love is God. God is the One pretending to be the many.

Inner awakenings lead to outer service to others.

Religion is based on someone else's mystical experience. Spirituality is based on your own mystical experience.

The war between religion and atheism is irrelevant to spirituality. Internally, we are all the same. Externally, we should allow for differences.

Both religion and atheism do themselves a disservice by ignoring or discounting spirituality. It is the point of view that could end their ongoing conflict. They are differing points of view that spirituality transcends. They both argue over the chaff while leaving the wheat on the ground.

Choose to have choices.
　　　　　　D.L.

Random Notes VI

To follow a religion and engage in its ritual and ceremony without reaching a spiritual level is to partake of an organization that has much to offer but is not likely to lead to enlightenment (epiphany). To pursue science (humanism) and to declare that only that which is detectable by the five senses is of value and proof of life is not only arrogant but falls short of exploring the entire human being.

To become steeped in religious ritual, sacred texts and exclusive esoterica is to "miss the mark" of the meaning behind sacred writings. Siddartha, Jesus and other sages (prophets) did not request that religions be formed around their teachings. They just offered their insights, wisdom and lessons that others might learn from them and thereby liberate themselves from suffering.

We have six senses. To deny the worth of one (the sixth) leads to an incomplete understanding of the human being. We have all experienced déjà vue, a hunch and (most importantly) love. Science requires that things be logical; make sense intellectually. These things do not make sense. They need to be felt to be known. This is the realm of the sixth sense; the intuition.

To ignore the awe and wonder of creation; of the universe – something out of nothing – What kind of sense does that make? Our inner life force, energy, source is as real (if not more real) than or 3-dimensional, physical world of duality. Quantum mechanics supports a view of our "outer" world as being truly non-physical, in flux and subject to the law of change (temporary).

Our "inner" world, rooted firmly in the present, is becoming recognized as eternal, real and not subject to change. Life, in total, can be of great value and worthy of scientific inquiry and, simultaneously, worthy of awe and wonder on a spiritual (not religious) level.

"You are the light you go towards."

Anonymous

Apples & Oranges

Religion and spirituality are like apples and oranges. They each have a different area of interest: a different area of expertise –

Religion is exclusive. It creates an "us" and a "them". Spirituality is inclusive. It says that all life is precious and equal.

Religion is filled with ritual and ceremony. Spirituality is spontaneous and creative.

Religion makes you dependent upon it – for comfort, for information, for salvation and more. Spirituality makes you independent of everything.

Religion has a hierarchy; from the most important and most revered to the least important and least revered. Spirituality has no hierarchy…all are equal.

Religion is taught. No one is born knowing about religion. Since they're taught, religions can teach anything they want. Spirituality is known, intuitively. It cannot be taught; it must be felt.

Religion is usually about God. Spirituality is not about anything…It is a direct, personal relationship with God.

Religion can be a comfort or a cause for discomfort, in this 3-dimensional, physical world of duality. Spirituality offers a way to transcend this world.

Religion can be a support system and a social and moral guidepost for the physical body and all external to it. Spirituality is the path to the inner world.

Religion is concerned with the divinity without. Spirituality is concerned with the divinity within.

Religion puts information in you. Spirituality helps you uncover what is already within you.

Religion needs followers. Spirituality needs nothing more than for you to lead yourself.

Choose carefully – From each according to its design; its purpose. Render unto religion that which belongs to religion. Render unto spirituality that which belongs to spirituality. They need not be adversaries. Let apples be apples and oranges be oranges.

We are not only enough…
We are all there is.
D.L.

Gnostic Notes

Gnostic Christianity is intuitive, inclusive and independent (much like Buddhism and other Eastern teachings). Gnosticism was popular and a contemporary of Orthodox Christianity in the early first century. Of the twenty-four original gospels, only four were adopted by orthodox Christianity (325 AD) and the rest by Gnostic Christianity.

Gnosis is Greek for knowledge. The opposite is agnostic (without the knowledge). There is no sin and no (need for) salvation, only ignorance and gnosis. "Whoever achieves gnosis is no longer a Christian, but a Christ." To truly know yourself, your true self, is to know God, which is enlightenment. Self and divine are identical. Enlightenment brings equality with Jesus.

Spiritual writings are written "in spirit". One with gnosis is expected to express his own perceptions, in his own words...writing, painting, poetry, etc. Gnosis transcends the church's authority because it is composed of direct access to God (a name given to the force recognized with a spiritual awakening).

Through the body, the soul experiences lust, desire, passion, anger and other forms of suffering. The only way out of suffering is to realize the truth about humanity's place and destiny in the universe. The truth can only be found within...a direct, personal experience. Jesus leads souls out of this world into enlightenment. The true church is invisible, not physical and it is inclusive.

Desire and attachment cause suffering. Acceptance and unconditional love transcends all suffering.
　　　　　　　D.L.

Gnostic Timeline

200 BCE – 200 CE, The Essenes (ascetic Jews in Israel) wrote the Dead Sea Scrolls

30 CE, Jews following Jesus (Joshua), a Jew

280-330 CE, gospels of Judas…he receives enlightenment

325 CE, the Council of Nicea; Emperor Constantine and the high priests choose the four gospels and quell remaining twenty. They try to destroy the Gnostics, who believe in internal enlightenment, for all and do not follow ritual and ceremony and the hierarchy of orthodox Christianity.

The four gospels chosen (Mathew, Mark, Luke and John) of the new Testament were not written by these four apostles. They were written by others, many years after the apostles lived.

1886 CE, gospel of Peter found. He has three figures ascending in the Resurrection.

1896 CE, gospel of Mary is shown to be a true disciple and a leader of the apostles. It was written approximately 220 CE.

1945 CE, 52 gospels (Gnostic) found. Written between 2nd and 4th century CE. From Jesus and other prophets and spiritual leaders. Called the Dead Sea Scrolls, found at Nag Hammadi in Israel. Jesus not unique in that "all can be one with the father"…"All are sons of God". God is within, waiting to be uncovered. Personal connection to God.

In the gospel of Thomas there are no miracles, no religion and no ceremony…opnly the sayings of Jesus.

Before everything else…know yourself: know where you come from and where you are going. "Light the lamp within you. The kingdom of God is within."-Jesus. The kingdom symbolizes a state of transformation. The kingdom of God is here, now.

> *"We're all leaves on the same tree."*
>
> Anonymous-(Native American)

Religion
1. Gives a place a sense of community
2. Can help educate
3. Can be a moral guidepost
4. Can raise funds for a worthy cause
5. Can be a support system
6. Can be a great help in times of disaster
7. Can offer counseling
8. Can be a path to enlightenment

* Spirituality and religion are not the same.
* Religions are usually begun by people who have not had a spiritual awakening.
* Meditation (formal and informal) is the usual path to enlightenment.

Differences between religion and spirituality

Religion is exclusive. It creates an "us" and a "them".
Spirituality is inclusive...all life is special, precious.

Religion is steeped in ritual and ceremony.
Spirituality is spontaneous and devoid of ritual and ceremony.

Religion offers dependency on others to intervene between you and your God.
Spirituality offers independence through direct contact with God.

Religion's God can get angry and be disappointed in you.
Spirituality's God in unconditional love.

Religion's God can crave obedience and loyalty. Spirituality's God does not need your obedience or loyalty.

You may never get the religious God's approval.
Spirituality's God always approves because God does not judge.

Religion's God holds out the promise of salvation. Spirituality's God reveals there's no need for salvation.

Religion's God can encourage a fear of death. Spirituality's God shows death to be a natural part of life...not to be feared.

Religion's God can offer the possibility of a hellish afterlife.
Spirituality's God assures you that hell is only here on earth.

Religion's God can focus on your weaknesses and flaws.
Spirituality's God focuses on your inner beauty.

Religion's God can generate competition. Spirituality's God generates cooperation.

Religion's God separates you and your creator. Spirituality's God unites you with your creator.

Religion's God is apart from you. Spirituality's God shows you and God to be one.

Trust your heart and intuition.

D.L.

Choice Number Three

People throughout the world and throughout history are given a choice of religion or atheism. There is a third choice...spirituality. Most people think religion when they hear the word spirituality. They are not the same. Most, if not all, religions are created around an individual's spiritual awakening...a mystical experience. Without spirituality there would be no religion.

Yet, even though religion starts with an epiphany, in many cases, it loses sight of its origins and overshadows the spiritual awakening with ritual and ceremony. Spirituality is not only a third choice of paths...It is the most important of all choices. It is the reason why we are here. It is our destiny.

You can become aware of your connection to a larger entity, source, energy, etc. and give it a name you're comfortable with...other than God, so there's no need to denounce God...It's only a word. Allah, cosmic consciousness, universal force, IT, nature are all only words for something nameless. So name away until you find a label you're comfortable with.

The energy source is the same throughout the universe and it is formless and nameless. So, choose a name (other than God) and a form you find acceptable (other than an old man with a beard) and learn to be comfortable with being more than your five senses.

There's no need for humanism and spirituality to be at odds. Spirituality is nonsectarian; not a religion. You can be spiritual without being religious (Albert Einstein). You can be one with all that is. In fact, you can be all that is, period.

Science and its usually accompanying humanism split with religion around the time of the Renaissance in Europe. Science and spirituality need not ever split. Spirituality can bridge the gap between them. It can do this because it is not religion. It can, however, enhance both science and religion. Whatever unites with spirituality gets better.

There is more to us than meets our five senses and our physical bodies – ideas, creativity, thoughts, feelings, intuition and love to name a few. Religion needs spirituality to flesh it out and to add substance to its ritual and ceremony. Spirituality is the Zen in Zen Buddhism. Spirituality is the faith that subatomic particles really exist in this 3-dimensional world. Quantum physics has faith that there is a unifying force in the universe. Unconditional love is the force behind everything. It is the real "God" particle.

Having faint that something undetectable by the five senses exists in no way diminishes science. On the contrary, this sort of faith leads to breakthroughs in science. Spirituality and faith is knowing; sensing something unseen, yet felt, as real. We are more than thinking chunks of meat. We are in touch with our higher selves.

Mother Theresa was not saintly because of her ritual and ceremony. Her greatness came from her self-actualized love…her spirituality.

Don't alienate yourself for your (energy) source – unconditional love out of fear that this would diminish your scientific creativity. Just because you have no use for ritual, ceremony, politics and power should not mean turning your back on spirituality…"Don't throw the baby out with the bathwater".

Be an intellect. Be a life-affirming intellect. Be a wise, old Einstein. Spirituality puts the civil in civilization. Dump the chaff but keep the wheat. Wed the best of science with the best of that which is beyond the physical and , as Voltaire said: "Have the best of all possible worlds."

Brilliant intellect without soul is shallow at best and dangerously isolated and angry at worst. With the combination of humanistic intellectuality and spirituality you get a refined, civil, empathetic, moral science that makes MRI's but not bombs, cancer treatments but not napalm, cures and comforts but doesn't "shock and awe".

With unconditional love in your heart you can be a brilliant scientist with no religion. With compassion in psyche you can give free reign to your intellectual capacities. With unconditional love and compassion as your moral yardstick you can turn your back on (orthodox) religion and open your heart to life…all life. Being the best you you can be means in all areas, even those undetectable by the five senses including those known only to your intuition and heart.

There is a beautiful, peaceful, loving, non-threatening part of each of us, deep inside just waiting to get out and enhance all that it touches. Letting it our is a win-win situation for you and for the world. It is the best in all of us and, it is in all of us.

Forgive, forget and move on.
D.L.

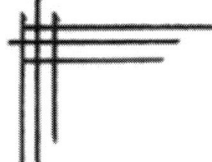

TWO MONKS

Tanzan and Ekido, were walking and came upon a swift-moving stream. A lovely young woman was standing by the stream, crying. "Why are you crying?" asked the elder of the two monks. "Because I can't cross the stream…I can't swim and don't want to get my clothes wet." "I'll take you across the stream," said the elder monk, scooping her up into his arms. After he put her safely down on the other side of the stream, she went one way and the two monks went another. After several hours, the young monk could contain himself no longer, and said: "How could you pick up that woman? Don't you know that monks are not allowed to touch women?" The elder said: "Are you still carrying that woman? I put her down hours ago.

Anonymous

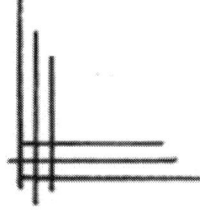

At the root of all religions and at the heart of spirituality lies the Golden Rule. Practice this every day, every chance you get, and you'll have no need of enlightenment.

D.L.

Random Notes VII

The world is not so much "out there" as it is "in here; in you". You and your outer world are interdependent. How the world is is not how you see it...How you see it (create it) is how the world is.

Mindfulness helps you understand this. Mindfulness is nonjudgmental awareness, which leads to self-knowing. It helps you to be present and awake in the here and now. You have to pay attention to your life as if it mattered. Then, you awaken to your own divinity and beauty within. This is the beginning of true wisdom. Knowledge comes from without. Wisdom comes from within.

Turn within and get to know yourself. As Socrates said: "The unexamined life is not worth living". As you become intimately familiar with yourself, you learn to accept yourself with kindness and compassion. With this new awareness you can change your karma; your fate. The more you know yourself, the more capable of healing yourself and, ultimately, of loving yourself. Follow the path of peace, love and silence within.

"The best meditation is no meditation" holds true for the life you are meant to live. When your life becomes your meditation, there's no need for "formal" meditation...unless that is already a part of your life. All meditation leads to liberation from suffering. Now you can be merged with the present moment, free of expectations. This is Zen's original mind.

Awareness of life leads to pure awareness: being life itself. "What you are looking for is who is looking", - St. Francis. Be present without attachment. Don't be this or that or something else. Just be. You, now, in this moment. Be who and where you are. Trust your heart and intuition...and your nonjudgmental mind. Be awake, alert and without thought. This is liberation from suffering.

Your journey is from point A to point A...from here to here. But, with a new understanding of here.

Instead of suffering with sensory impotence – to look without seeing, to listen without hearing and, ultimately, to touch without feeling; a learned disease of isolation and pain, you can go on to a life of unity, peace, happiness, health, goodness, beauty and love. All this comes with conscious awareness of your connection to something greater than yourself and your connection to others.

Learn from your past,
plan for your future,
but live in the present.
D.L.

Random Notes VIII

We humans are sentient...we think, and we are conscious; even self-conscious. Because of this, we are the point and purpose of creation – We are how the cosmos becomes conscious of itself.

We are an essential part of the cosmic plan. The ultimate goal of the power (God, source, energy, etc.) behind the universe is to unfold and evolve...without limits. The universe is conscious, creative and ever-changing.

The "divine plan" unfolds through each of us. This gives our lives meaning and purpose, on the individual and collective levels. Consciousness must evolve and grow. This is its purpose. It does this with and through us.

Without us to be conscious of and to bear witness to all of creation, there is no creation. We exist so all (physical and non-physical) can exist. The non-physical includes love, inspiration, creativity, compassion, beauty, intuition, truth and enlightenment. The physical is the entire universe.

Awareness, intelligence, creativity and soul are all unseen, yet real. Awareness (mindfulness) is the key to personal transformation; to awakening your "higher self".

The universe (one turned on itself) is us, contemplating it (us).

We and all creation are One.

The person you seek is the same person seeking you...There is No "other" person.

Our intuition (feelings); our sixth sense, is our path to spirituality.

Have faith in yourself. Lose your ego and gain the world. Each day is a new world and can see a new you.

Get involved in your "right" activities.

When you get lost in your life, as it is happening, you are awake, alert and without thought. This is meditation...the true path to enlightenment. This is what it means to be "born again". Your first birth is physical (external). Your second birth is spiritual (internal).

Follow the "Six-Step Path" to enlightenment. – 1. Observe yourself without judgment. 2. Forgive yourself and others. 3. Accept what you observe. 4. Love yourself unconditionally. 5. Awaken from your dream. 6. Celebrate life forever.

"Life is like an onion —
you peel it layer by
layer,
and sometimes you cry."
Carl Sandburg

Random Notes IX

The goal: to become one with the universe...to wake up

Now that you're an adult, it is time to stop blaming others for who you are and time to decide who you want to be now.

Accept the impermanence of life and who you are. Forgive all and focus on the present...and awaken.

May your peace with the fact that you cannot be anything other than who you are. Just be the best you you can be...from moment to moment.

We do not live for ourselves, alone. We all have gifts and talents to share. With this sharing we make the world a better place for us having been here. "Bring happiness by entering a room, not by leaving it."

You have the right; the obligation to live and to write your story. So, take the time and make the effort to "grow into yourself." Don't die before you have begun to live.

Real beauty is not what we're born with. Real beauty is what we become.

"If you are restless, something spiritual needs attention. Something in all of us strains for fulfillment." If you want to know peace, contentment, joy and love, you must nourish your soul.

We manufacture our own suffering and we must learn to transcend this suffering. All things are impermanent. Clinging, desire, attachment and...resisting change cause suffering. Everything changes. Live in the present.

"Life is what you make it – always has been, always will be." – Grandma Moses

Religion makes us aware of God. Spirituality allows us to transform our lives and give it purpose. It puts us in touch with God. Religion gives a guide…spirituality makes you your own guide. Religion is a bridge to God…spirituality is union with God. "With spirituality you embrace the world, melt into God and become the love that is God." Spirituality takes us beyond religion to awareness of the sacredness in all…here and now, always. Religion is about God. Spirituality is a personal connection to God. Our essence, source, etc. is the subject of religion. This essence leads us to the sacredness of all life. The sacred, the secular, the material, the spiritual are all part of the One. Religion itself is not sacred…It is a path to the sacred…a path, not the destination.

May you learn to accept your goodbyes as you do your hellos.
　　　　　D.L.

Random Notes X

Our source or essence wants to know itself. That's why it asks: "Who am I?" It wishes to grow, expand and create. Why? Because that is its nature. Our essence is constantly creating itself. You are a unique way for the universe to be conscious of itself. This is an eternal genesis. The universe created creators...us, like itself. The universe wants to "live and breathe through us."

When you and your source are one, is the world in you or are you in the world? The world "out-there" is not disconnected from you...it is you. I, we are it and it is us. So, are we in the world or is the world in us?

Bhakti yoga leads to God through love. Raj yoga leads to God through meditation.

Relax into the rhythm of your life.

Suffering is pain that we hold on to because we have denied it. Suffering comes from not knowing who you are.

The ego wants to be number one.

Choose spontaneity over old beliefs. Spontaneity leads to "choiceless awareness". We can only make choices in the present.

Being fully present means being fully open to receive, from moment to moment, which means being free to give back, creatively, every moment.

Life (appears to) goes from unity to duality to unity.

God inhabits a world beyond the five senses. This world is perceived as light. You are the light you go towards.

When you are aware of yourself without being attached to any particular age, you've found the observer within; the one who doesn't come and go.

Karma equals action. Being equals no action. Yet, creativity is your middle name.

The now is when linear time is nonexistent. It is ever fresh and changeless. Focus, focus, focus…don't wander.

Good impulses and latent talents die from lack of use. Love does not grow if suppressed.

It's easy to be yourself when you're not self-conscious.

D.L.

Random Notes XI

Adam and Eve were evicted from the Garden of Eden (Paradise) for gaining knowledge and losing their innocence. They felt sinful (an illusion).

It took all that has happened in your life to get you here, now. Be happy with no reason. You are just where you're supposed to be. Trust your heart and intuition. Your spiritual evolution to higher consciousness, beauty, truth, art & love is in progress. Expansion of consciousness is the divine plan (unity with God) and you are a major part of the plan. In fact, you are the plan.

You are the writer, director, producer and main character in your own movie. But, unbeknownst to you, the movie doesn't control you. You control the movie. You are the author of everything that happens to you.

Go deep, quietly, to find happiness, wakefulness and mindfulness (awareness). Be awake, alert and without thought. Nothing is more fascinating than finding out who you really are and what you are really about. Most people only know what they've been told, taught at school, in church or from their family. The need to conform to all this teaching creates a fear of breaking free.

"The voice of freedom tells you what you want to do. The voice of fear tells you what you'd better do. You get to be whoever you want to be and to do whatever you want to do". When freed from all past influences and living spontaneously, in the present, you get to see, and be, the real you.

Zen is waking up to your everyday life and living it fully with complete concentration.

D.L.

Random Notes XII

You are programmed for success. By doing nothing, you can break through; wake up to your true self.

Thinking and wanting keep you from being in the (eternal) now. Judging also keeps you from this moment. You only need to be aware and awake...awake, alert and without thought, lost in your life, as it is happening. This is all you need do.

All that is impermanent is illusion. All that changes is illusion. All that has a beginning has an end. All that has a birth has a death. All that is detectable by the five senses is temporary. That which is detectable by the sixth sense; the intuition, - unconditional love, is the only thing that is eternal and, therefore, real. It does not change. This three-dimensional, physical world of duality is ruled by the law of change. Unconditional love is free of this rule. Unconditional love is eternal.

Don't run from suffering or bad news. Embrace it, as you would good news and happiness. Be open to all your life, as it is happening...warts and all. Live your life, moment by moment and you will be in touch with the divinity within; your source.

Be true to yourself, and you will be happy. Observe yourself without judgment and you create a safe, welcoming atmosphere. Now, your true, hidden, gifts and talents can emerge and blossom. Happiness prevails. Good for you and good for the world.

The past is over and the future has yet to begin. The only time you can live is now. Pay attention to your now, however it is. Your true self is hidden in the now. Your well being and happiness are in this moment.

"The only meditation is no meditation." Let your life be your (informal) meditation. When you meditate formally, there is a you to meditate. When your life is your meditation, you get lost in the moment and lose yourself to the now...there is no you at all. You are awake, alert and without thought. When you and your activity are one, there is no you. Then you are ready for enlightenment.

Don't seek. Just be. Don't strive. There is nothing to get and no one to get it. There is nothing to prove and nothing to be gained. You are already worthy and, remember, programmed for success. When you stop striving, stop wanting, stop feeling separate and incomplete, stop being attached, stop doubting...you are ready.

You are perfect within. The light you go towards is you. You are the seeker and the sought, the question and the answer, the lost and the found. You are all there is. Forget desires. Forget attachments. Forget your earthly self and remember your spiritual self. Observe without judgment and all will be revealed. And, while doing all of this...be kinder; to yourself and to others.

Be mindful of all that is without you and all that is within you. Watch even your thoughts. Don't resist your thoughts...just watch them. They will come and they will go. Concentrated, non-judgmental observation.

See the world without judgment, without condemnation, as it is. Become aware of the physical world, other people and yourself, especially your thoughts...without judgment. Do this now and wake up to your true self. It is not detectable by your five senses. You'll have to use your sixth sense – your intuition. This is the part of you that feels. This is the part of you that knows love.

Enlightenment is when you are not. Enlightenment and ego cannot co-exist. Enlightenment and you cannot co-exist. As you (ego, I) disappear, enlightenment arises. Don't think. Just be.the best you you can be, in this very moment.

As Siddartha said: "Be in this world, but not of it. Cling to nothing and resist nothing." In this way; being totally involved, in your life, as it is happening, you awaken from your dream and discover your true, inner, self.

Be content with what is, now. Don't try to change anything. Just let it be. You and your activity as one. No thought, just being. No judgment, just acceptance of that is. Mindfulness – a moment-to-moment, non-judgmental awareness. This behavior leads to finding your true self, which is "hidden in plain sight".

"Be yourself; everyone else is already taken."

Oscar Wilde

REMINDER

Each of us has certain gifts that lead to doing work that best suits those gifts. Do what is right for you – If you love cooking, mahjongg and gardening, then get involved with cooking, mahjongg and gardening. Get totally involved in these and all other activities that are "right" for you; such as sitting, walking, swimming, meditating, etc. Be involved in all that feels appropriate to you, for you.

How do you know which activities are right for you? If you lose track of time during an activity then it's probably right for you. From the minute you wake up in the morning until you close your eyes at night, embrace whatever comes your way; completely involved without expectations.

Be the best you you can be, 24/7, without judgment. – How well you perform these "right" activities is irrelevant. If you must compare your performance, compare you now with you before…but not to anyone else. Do this, and you will be living the life you are meant to live…your life. You are programmed for success; as long as you do what feels right for you.

Accept good news, bad news and all news in between. Embrace it, accept it and get through it and get on with your life. Your life will flow in a natural rhythm, without suffering. There will be sad times – people you're close to will get sick, move away and die. Severe weather will strike and stocks will fall, but there will be no lingering suffering if you live your life as it is happening.

Living this way, spontaneously, honestly and unselfconsciously, you'll wake up to the fact that you're part of something greater than yourself. In fact, you are that thing greater than yourself. You destiny as a human being, to follow your heart and intuition, will be realized. You life will be the life you're meant to live and you will be one with all that is. You will know a life of peace, love and joy. And, you will want to celebrate this life by serving others.

Love isn't blind....It's forgiving.
D.L.

Happiness

Assuming we all want to be happy; which includes peace of mind, consider the following-

* If individual happiness is dependent on material success, then the more money and material wealth one has, the greater should be one's happiness. Compare Howard Hughes or Bernie Madoff with Martin Luther King, Jr.

* If individual happiness is dependent on the extent and force of one's religious leanings, than the more extreme one's religious views, the greater should be one's happiness. Compare Osama Ben Laden with Gandhi.

* If individual happiness is in proportion to one's (culturally supported) idea of good looks, then the more attractive one is, the happier one should be. Compare Marilyn Monroe with Mother Theresa.

* If individual happiness is dependent on one's intellectual prowess, then the higher the IQ, the happier the individual. Think Edward Teller (physicist)-(Dr. Strangelove)
compared to Confucius.

* If individual happiness is dependent on one's weight, then the thinner one is the happier one should be. Compare Burl Ives with Charles Manson.

* If individual happiness is dependent on the state of one's physical health, then the physically healthier one is the happier one should be. Think Michael Jackson.

* If individual happiness is the result of recognition by one's peers, then the most popular, lauded, decorated and celebrated of us should be the happiest. Think Joan Crawford, Jim Baker and Richard Nixon.

* If individual happiness is dependent on the level of our talents, then the most talented of us should be the happiest of us. Compare Beethoven with Tiny Tim.

None of these qualities seems to be the key to happiness. The guarantee of happiness due to these positions is a non sequitur of major proportions. We all know people (personally) and of people in the public eye who possess one of more of these positions. We also know that happiness does not necessarily accompany them due to these positions.

Happiness seems to be the result of an internal mindset. Therefore, we are in control of our level of happiness. Our attitude is everything in this matter. "I think most people are about as happy as they've made up their minds to be." – Abe Lincoln

How to live:
1. Sing as if no one is listening.
2. Dance as if no one is watching.
3. Work as if you don't need the money.
4. Love like nobody has ever hurt you.
5. Live as if this was paradise on Earth.

Alfred D. Souza

Creativity

Creativity is the nectar of the gods. When it flows, it's the adrenalin in your veins. When bathed in it's all-consuming fragrance, you know down to your bones that you're part of something greater than yourself. You lose all track of time. Your need for rest, for food, for sleep and especially, for thought, vanish.

The artist, graced with creative inspiration, makes paintings, writes music, choreographs dance, produces new shapes and writes books, because of this inner force. The inspiration (to be in spirit) needs a creative outlet on the physical plane, to express itself - The inspirational force is formless and so needs people to give it form. Without creative inspiration, nothing happens. Without the artist, nothing happens. Without a witness to the creation, the audience, there's little point in creating. All three are necessary in the creative process.

Whether you paint, sculpt, write books, make music, dance, make crafts, design buildings, take photographs, write poems, act, cook, garden, make films or are active in science, you relish the moment when inspiration strikes. You can feel it. It's time to move, to make, to do. You will not be distracted. When your muse calls, the physical world disappears and your focus narrows to the task at hand. Words and forms and sounds and design elements must all be assembled in balanced harmony so that beauty can be born.

All thought vanishes in an energetic frenzy that will not rest until all creative efforts are resolved into a wholly satisfying result. This is not the time for critique. Not the time for thought. This is the time to surrender, totally, to the direction from within. Like a cork in a swift-moving stream, you are willingly tossed this way and that, at the whim of the work. And, never forget-this is work...glorious work, all encompassing work, welcome work. Work that lets you know what it means to be fully alive, in the moment...100% involved and 0% attached to the results.

A thinking artist puts pencil to paper and makes marks. The inspired artist caresses the paper with graphite, lovingly and maneuvers the material to create genius on the two-dimensional level. Whether words or paint strokes or sounds, when the work is done, if only for that day, you are drained, but grateful to have been part of the creative equation. Exhausted, now comes pleasurable rest.

The truth and beauty of great art can be felt. People are moved by the legitimate expression of inner forces. That sharing of honest form can lead to tears of joy or tears of sadness...whichever the artist conveyed.

The harmonious combination of just the right measured elements and a regularly practiced technique – the proper balance of parts, the just right scale of proportion, the perfect word or sound or movement at just the right moment is beauty of the first order.

No need for instruction on how to react. When in the presence of honest, true creation, of any media, the heart knows how to feel. The pulse races in harmony with the creation. The appropriate applause comes naturally. The viewer and the viewed, or read, or sung merge in a willing dance of appreciation. Smiles spread and beam, bursting with feeling.

The artist creates from an inner urge to express. The force within gets to channel itself, through the artist, to become a physical creation. This formless power has been given form. The viewer is pleased to share in this creation. Force, artist, audience – a win, win, win situation of the first magnitude. All are satisfied.

The writer, the content and the reader are all necessary in this celebration of creative activity. All have a part to play. Each must be open to receive its offering. The force is grateful for a path to follow. The artist is grateful for the inspiration and the chance to use his/her talents. The audience is grateful to bear witness to truth and beauty.

Creativity is a fundamental human expression. It puts the civil in civilization. It is, ultimately, why we are here. Without us, the sound of the tree falling in the forest is lost. It is our destiny as a species to listen to our inner voices. We are obliged to receive what is offered in the loving spirit in which it is offered. We are grateful to be a channel for our inner force and to allow it to flow through us to others.

Inspiration, creator, audience. Sometimes we are one, sometimes another, but we're all part of the creative equation. Creativity is the breath of life. We couldn't live without it.

Your destiny is to awaken to a direct, non-intellectual, experience of reality…something greater than yourself.

—D.L.

Inspirational Writing

Inspirational writing stimulates, arouses, excites, educates, exhilarates, activates.

We're all born with flaws and weaknesses. We're also born with gifts and talents. We discover which activities are right for us by doing what makes us happy, what excites us, what grabs our attention to the point where we lose track of time. When we allow ourselves to participate in what is a right activity for us we soar. "It's never too late to what you might have been." – George Eliot.

For some, a right activity is dance, sports, gardening, cooking, painting, etc...Runners run, painters paint and writers write. It's what we do. It's what we are. If your right activity is writing; in particular inspirational writing, then this is what you should be doing. Write because it makes you happy. Write because you have to. But write. To do anything well requires effort, work. Whatever is your "right" activity. Do it now. Do it often. As Nike says: "Just do it."

Inspirational writings are stories that inspire. They highlight people overcoming adversity or people reaching new levels of understanding. This is my kind of writing. I write on spirituality. My prose, my poetry, my aphorisms all inspire people to be the best they can be...not the best in the world, just their personal best at that time.

Believe in yourself. As Henry Ford said: "If you think you can or can't – you're right." Or, as Zora Neale Hurston said: "There is no agony like having an untold story inside you." Let your writing give people hope and courage and the strength to endure.

Louis Pasteur said: "Fortune favors the prepared mind." Be prepared. Be ready for inspiration's arrival. Write on in spite of negative critiques and rejections. Keep writing. "No one can lower your self esteem without your approval."-

Eleanore Roosevelt. Follow your dreams, your bliss. As Ralph Waldo Emerson said: "to be yourself in a world that is constantly trying to make you something else is the greatest accomplishment." If inspirational writing is your goal, your passion, then pursue it with all your might.. "What ever you can do or dream you can, begin it. Boldness has genius, power and magic in it." Goethe.

"Your work should be love made visible."-Kahlil Gibran. And it will be if it is from the heart. Write what you know and write what you love. When your work honestly and concisely expresses you, you are doing the right thing at the right time.

Searching for God with your mind is like watching a movie with your elbow
D.L.

Relationships – Do's and Don'ts

Above all...Be kinder...kinder and gentler. When you're in agreement then be in agreement. When you disagree, then disagree. No anger. No nastiness. No attacking. And, don't expect to always be in agreement...Don't demand to be in sync. Be truthful (to your own self) and honest about where you are to your partner.

This is not a competition – so don't make it one. Don't make it a case of winners and losers. Allow difference of opinion to have its day in court. Let love be your weapon of choice...unconditional love – no judgments, only tenderness and respect. Be a "them" with breathing room.

Believe in your ability to change for the better. The same goes for others. And, be patient. All things pass. Whether in a relationship with a friend, a mate, a sibling, one of your children or any other family member, business partner, etc., change happens...in most cases. Don't demand success every time – "Some days you get the bear and some days the bear gets you. Some days chicken, some days feathers."

Never forget: You're programmed for success. Believe in yourself and in goodness. Everything that's happened to you from day one was necessary to get you to where you are today. The same goes for others. We all have lessons to learn.

There is much in this world to fear and loath. But, there is so much more to love and be grateful for. Accept your goodbyes as you do your hellos. Allow for and encourage growth...in self and others.

We all make mistakes. It's only human. Learning from our mistakes is what makes them worthwhile. Cherish and learn from your past and be inspired by your plans for the future but live in the present – 100% involved in your life and 0% attached to results. Don't fight change.

You're only half of a relationship so there's no need to thank or blame. Just be the best you you can be at the time. No anger. Just unconditional love, patience and kindness. This will make you part of the solution…not part of the problem.

kindness, love, a smile and
laughter...
Give them away and
they return soon
after.
D.L.

We are what we observe...

As stated by the law of conservation of mass, "matter can neither be created nor destroyed". We come from (cosmic) dust and to dust we shall return. We, being made up of these cosmic dust particles, are as old as the universe. We are old and we are sentient. And, being sentient, we are conscious and as consciousness, we are self-aware.

Self-awareness leads to questions – Who am I? Why am I here? Is the universe random? We are not accidents nor are we random creations of nature. We have purpose – Like true artists, we give form and meaning to the universe.

Take away our five senses and we would have no knowledge of the physical world of three dimensions. Without our consciousness, nothing is. Quantum mechanics supports this...With no one to observe, no physical event happens.

We are not just any minute part of a vast cosmos. Without us and our awareness, there is no cosmos. We don't live in it. It lives in us. "The world is not so much as we find it but how we make it." We and the universe are mutually interdependent.

When we focus on something, we and it become (temporarily) real. When we focus on nothing (as in meditation), we are not and the world is not. The world begins and ends with us. While our left brain sees itself as an isolated "I", our right brain sees the (whole) universe and "seamlessly aligns with this observation."

In this 3-D physical world of duality there is no "out there". There is only us creating/observing. We are anything but static. We are like a swiftly-moving stream...in a constant state of flux, active...a process, not a thing.

As we think, so the world is. Our search for our selves is the cosmo's search for itself. We are "thinking, reasoning components of the universe." We are part of something greater than ourselves. We are one with the universe. We are it and it is us. All is One.

Through us the universe becomes conscious of itself.

D.L.

Meditation

When your search for the meaning of life can no longer be handled by the intellect, you're ready for spirituality; which is best handled by your intuition.

The purpose of traditional, formal meditation; be it yoga (Raj yoga leads to God through meditation.), transcendental, zazen or some other form, is to teach you how to be awake, alert (mindful) and without thought...to be 100% in the moment. Being grounded in the (your) now allows your true self, with all your gifts and talents, to emerge and to blossom. Form meditations involve ritual, ceremony and a great deal of practice.

However, you can also live your life in such a way that it, your life, becomes your meditation… "The best meditation is no meditation." This is living your life, as it happens. Just as you get lost in a movie, a book, a hobby and all "right" activities for you, you get lost in your life. Please see my "Six-Step Path" for this informal meditation. Involved in this way, you are ripe for enlightenment. Just stay focused on the present moment. The power and glory of self-realization through meditation is waiting for you.

Love and be loved.
All else is unnecessary.
　　　　　D.L.

Made in the USA
Charleston, SC
30 December 2013